Garden of Eden

Plants of the Hebrew Bible

Gloria Abella Ballen

Garden of Eden

Plants of the Hebrew Bible

Gaon Books

Contents

Introduction	9
Paradise	11
The Five Most Mentioned Fruits in the Hebrew Bible	21
Other Plants in the Hebrew Bible	35
References	206
About the Author	207

Plants of the Hebrew Bible

Acacia	39	Durra	96	Olive tree	152
Almond	41	Ebony	99	Papyrus	155
Almug	42	Emmer	100	Pistachios	157
Aloe	45	Fig tree	102	Plane	158
Apple	47	Fig sycamore	105	Pomegranate	160
Apricot	48	Flax	107	Poplar	162
Balm	51	Frankincense	109	Poppy coronaria	165
Barley	53	Garlic	111	Quince	167
Bdellium	55	Gourd	113	Reed	168
Bean	56	Grapevine	115	Rocket	170
Boxthorn	58	Hemlock	116	Saffron	172
Black cumin	61	Henna	119	Sage, Judean	174
Bramble	62	Hyssop	121	Saltwort	176
Broom bush	64	Jujube, wild	122	Storax	178
Aromatic cane	66	Juniper	125	Tamarisk	181
Caper	71	Ladanum	126	Terebinth	183
Castor oil	73	Laurel	128	Thistle	185
Cedar	74	Leek	131	Sow Thistle	187
Chick-pea	77	Lentils	133	Thorn	189
Cinnamon	79	Lilies	135	Thorn camel	191
Citron	80	Mandrake	136	Thorn gundelia	193
Coriander	83	Manna	139	Tragacanth	195
Cotton	85	Melon	140	Walnut	196
Cucumber	86	Myrrh	142	Weed ridolfia	198
Cumin	89	Myrtle	145	Wheat	201
Cypress	91	Nard	147	Willow	203
Daffodil	93	Nettle	149	Wormwood	205
Date palm	95	Oak	151		

And the Lord God
caused trees to sprout from the earth that
were pleasing to look at and good for food.
The tree of life was in the middle of the
garden and the tree of knowledge
of good and bad.

Genesis 2:9

The man and woman
heard the sound of the Lord God
moving in the garden at the time
of the evening breeze, and they hid from Him
among the trees. The Lord God called to the man,
"Where are you?" He answered, "I heard the
sound of you in the garden, and I was afraid
because I was naked, so I hid."

Genesis 3:8-10

For David, Leon and Roni

INTRODUCTION

I remember walking through the luscious and colorful fields of the Savannah of Bogota, in South America, planted with many kinds of grasses and flowers and trees of big and small leaves, fruits, and seeds in a plethora of colors. It was a paradise.

In school we would make pen and ink drawings of plants that we collected on walks, and we pressed them between papers to dry and save, making annotations about each one in a notebook. We were taught this was the way the naturalists from the famous Royal Botanical Expedition to New Granada (1783-1816) had collected and recorded plants. In that Expedition the Spanish physician and naturalist José Celestino Mutis, a disciple of Linnaeus, had meticulously recorded the existence of more than 5,300 flora species with beautiful drawings.

As a child learning about the natural world that was my environment, I felt like a scientist/artist as I made drawing after drawing of plants. It was a happy and challenging experience in a world that seemed like Paradise to me. Later in my professional career, I drew from the magic of plants as an inspiration for abstract works in painting and ceramic sculpture. Now, I have returned to plants themselves as the subject, in this case as they appear in the Hebrew Bible (*Tanakh*).

The numinous metaphors of nature have always held special meaning for me, and the Bible offers beautiful examples such as the Tree of Life that granted immortality, the Tree of Knowledge of good and bad, and the burning bush where God first revealed Himself to Moses.

An angel of the Lord appeared to him like a fire burning out of a bush. The bush was on fire, but it was not being burned up.
Exodus 3:2

The burning bush has been associated with the *Rubus sanguineus,* or holy bramble (*petel kadosh*) a thorny bush with pink flowers and red berrys, related to the blackberry. It is not possible to scientifically identify the burning bush, since its meaning is not based on a natural reality but on the vision of God, (Gardner 2014:90) whose presence is repeatedly referred to as *"a flaming torch"* (Genesis 15:17), *"consuming fire"* (Deuteronomy 4:24), *"fiery flames"* (Psalms 104:4). This is a dramatic image of God's power that led the people of Israel out of Egypt as a pillar of fire.

Historically the plants of the Bible have been of great interest for botanical studies, for their medicinal qualities, for cooking, for building gardens, for inspiration, and as metaphors for teaching.

The Bible often provides both social and symbolic meanings for plants, but sometimes the ambiguity of language means that the species mentioned cannot be specifically identified. The Bible was written in Aramaic and Hebrew, it was first translated into Greek in the second century B.C.E., into Latin in the fourth century C.E., and later into the many languages of the world. As we will see, the story of those translations has affected our understanding of the plants.

In this book I include the Hebrew name and the Latin scientific name for each of the plants, as well as the common name in English. Along with the images, I include a biblical reference to the plant with my interpretation of the verse, based on the 1917 JPS translation. The text focuses on the five most mentioned plants: fig, grape vine, olive, date palm and pomegranate.

The generic Hebrew term for fruit (*peri*) is used throughout the Bible. In many cases the reference is to the olive, fig, or grape the three most important fruits to the Israelites after they left Egypt. Isaiah predicts that the descendants of Jacob will blossom and fill the world with fruit, making Israel a gift to the world.

In the days to come Jacob's descendants will take root, Israel will sprout and blossom, and they will fill the entire world with fruit.
Isaiah 27:6

The Hebrew word "seed" (*zera*) is regularly mentioned in reference to a grain crop, not being clear whether the reference is to wheat, barley, spelt or millet. Since wheat was the most highly esteemed and valuable, it was the most common seed. Wheat is clearly identified in many biblical verses: *"They have sown wheat and harvest thorns…"* (Jeremiah 12:13)

Wheat is also depicted in Egyptian monuments and apparently in the dream of Pharaoh, which Joseph was asked to interpret.

In another dream, I saw seven full and ripe clusters of grain growing on a stalk. Coming up behind them were seven other clusters shriveled, thin and damaged by the east wind.
Genesis 41:22-23

Seeds like coriander are identified in Exodus 16:31.

Israel called it manna. It was like a white coriander seed, and it tasted like a wafer made with honey.

For the Israelites it was specifically forbidden to mix seeds of various grains *"…you shall not sow your field with two kinds of seed…"* Leviticus 19:19

The Jewish historian Josephus in the first century C.E. described the land of Israel as "a garden of God" because of the beauty and lusciousness of the amazing variety of trees and orchards.

This harmony and beauty of plants, the plentiful seeds, fruit trees, herbs and grasses made the land a paradise.

Paradise

The notion of Paradise brings to mind a place of timeless harmony, beauty, luxury and contentment. Paradise, *Gan-Eden*, in Hebrew, often refers to a "higher place" a blissful, heavenly abode, a holy place for the righteous after death. In the Abrahamic tradition, Paradise is associated with "the Garden of Eden," the place of beauty and perfection before the transgression by Adam and Eve. It was the perfect state that will be brought back in the world to come (heaven).

> *The Lord God planted a garden in Eden to the east and placed there Adam who He had created. And the Lord God caused trees to sprout from the earth that were pleasing to look at and good for food. The Tree of Life was in the middle of the garden, and the tree of knowledge of good and bad.*
> Genesis 2:8-9

There were also instructions to be followed concerning the garden in Genesis 2:15-17

> *The Lord God took the man and put him in the garden of Eden to cultivate it and guard it. And the Lord God spoke to the man saying, "You may eat from any tree in the garden, except for the tree of knowledge of good and bad, you must not eat of it; for as soon as you eat it, you shall die.*

The Creation account mentions two trees that have supernatural qualities: the Tree of Life that granted immortality and the forbidden Tree of Knowledge of good and bad (*ra*). The first tree mentioned by name in Genesis is the fig tree when Adam and Eve used the leaves to make coverings for themselves when they realized their nakedness after eating from the Forbidden Tree.

> *Then, their eyes were opened, and they realized that they were naked, so they sewed fig leaves together and made loincloths for themselves.*
> Genesis 3:7

Elements of the Garden of Creation can be seen in the distant Ur of Abraham. The Sumerians believed in an original mound of creation. Other elements of the account of the Garden appear in Babylonian literature like the *Epic of Gilgamesh,* the king/hero who traveled to the garden of the gods which contained many species of trees, including a "plant of life", and semi-precious stones such as lapis-lazuli. Gilgamesh's story also had a snake that stole the essence of eternal life.

An Akkadian clay cylinder from 2100 B.C.E. depicts a man and a woman sitting on each side of a palm tree from which clusters of dates hang and behind them is a serpent. This cylinder is popularly known as "cylinder of the Temptation" (British Museum). This is not the Garden of Eden, but the allusion is suggestive.

In the Genesis narrative the Garden of Eden is described as a fertile place watered by various rivers:

A river flows out of Eden to water the garden, and it branches into four different streams. The name of the first is Pishon, the one that winds the entire land of Havilah, where gold is found. The gold of that land is good, and gum resin and lapis lazuli. The name of the second river is Gihon, the one goes through the entire land of Cush. The name of the third is Tigris, and this is the river that flows east of Asshur. The fourth river is the Euphrates.
Genesis 2:10-14

In Barton's *A Sketch of Semitic Origins*, 1902, the Semite conception of Paradise was like the fertile oases that are found in the deserts of the Middle East and North Africa. Babylon is famous for the gardens that apparently made it an urban paradise. Its people were urbane and literate, and we find reports of their gardens from written texts, pictorial sculpture, and archaeology.

In the Hebrew Bible, (*Tanakh*) the word *Pardes*, meaning orchard, is mentioned in three other places, more as a reference to specific orchards or fruit gardens than as a metaphor for high holy places.

We read in The Song of Songs 4:13,

Your shoots are an orchard of pomegranates, with all precious fruits, henna with spikenard plants.

In Ecclesiastes 2:5-6, Koheleth, son of king David in Jerusalem says:

I made orchards and parks, and I planted every kind of fruit trees in them. I made pools of water, to water the forest where the trees were growing.

And in Nehemiah 2:8

A letter to Asaph the keeper of the king's forest, for him to give me timber to make beams for the gates of the citadel of the temple, for the walls of the city, and for the house that I will occupy.

Jewish authorities are almost unanimous in claiming that there was a terrestrial as well as a celestial *Gan-Eden,* (Paradise) occasionally alluded to as *Olam Ha Ba*, the world to come.

In post-biblical Hebrew the mnemonic/anagram "PaRDeS" refers to the mystical Kabbalist philosophy that assigns four levels of understanding to the *Torah. P'shat, Remez, D'rash* and *Sod*. Each layer or meaning is deeper and more intense than the previous. *P'shat is* the simple literal understanding while *Sod* is the hidden, deeper mystical meaning. This acronym appeared for the first time in the writings of Moses de Leon in thirteenth century Spain as part of the *Zohar*, the book of Splendor.

PaRDeS, the mystical system of the four levels of understanding *Torah* becomes a parallel with the word *Pardes,* an orchard of trees and fruits.

The most famous *Pardes* story is about the experience of four first century rabbis, who entered *Pardes,* the Orchard Paradise. *Ben Azzai* looked and died; *Ben Zoma* looked and went mad; *Acher* destroyed the plants; *Akiva* entered in peace and departed in peace.

Entering the orchard, *Pardes,* in this story is a metaphor for the richness of the four levels of Torah meaning and understanding, and not synonymous with *Gan-Eden,* Garden of Eden or Paradise.

The Mystical Tree of Life

The Bible is also associated with the Tree of Life, *Etz Hayim,* as a source of wisdom. Adam and Eve were put in the Garden of Eden, *Gan-Eden,* a place of perfect beauty, fruitfulness and contentment. The central features of the garden were two fruit-bearing trees: one the Tree of Life and the other the Tree of Knowledge of good and bad. With this we start the botanical narrative of the Bible with the variety of trees from the olive to the date palm, acacia, and cedar of Lebanon among others. The references to these plants may be as symbols, metaphors, sources of food, protection, or inspiration. In Hosea 14:5-7 we read:

I will be like the dew to Israel.
He will blossom like the lily,
and send deep roots like a tree of Lebanon.
His branches will spread out,
and his beauty will be like the olive tree,
with fragrance like that of the tree of
Lebanon. People who sit in its shade will be
revived. They will revive like the grain,
and blossom like the vine. Their fragrance
will be like the wine of Lebanon.

In Kaballah, the Jewish mystical tradition, the Tree of Life refers to the well-known diagram illustrating the ten divine emanations or *sfirot*. The Tree of Life is also the title of a major work of Jewish mysticism by Rabbi Hayim Vital in the sixteenth century.

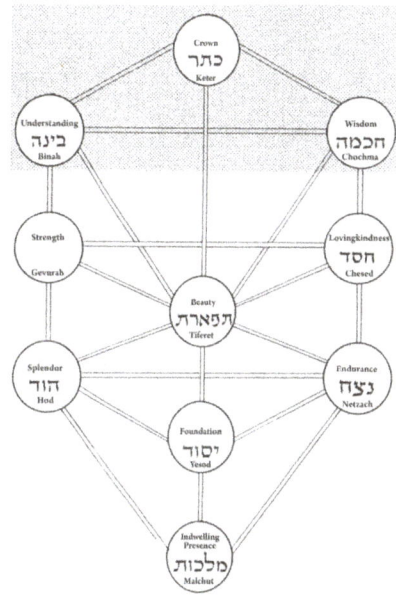

Kabbalistic Tree of Life

The Tree of Life as a metaphor for Torah comes from the book of Proverbs in 3:18:

She is a tree of life to those who hold her.
Happy is everyone who retains her.

Our mortality and the fleeting nature of human life is likened to vegetation which is vibrant one day, but soon passes, and Isaiah metaphorically compares it to grass:

All flesh is like grass, and all its glory is like the flowers of the field. Grass withers, flowers fade, because the breath of the Lord blows on it. Indeed people are like grass. Grass withers, flowers fade, but the word of our God stands forever.
Isaiah 40:6-8

The poets of the Bible saw rapid growth and the wickedness of their enemies as transient as flowers, as in Psalm 103:15: *he blooms as a flower of the field.*

The description of the menorah in the Bible, often translated as lampstand, seems botanical and perhaps was based, on a wild sage plant in bloom, commonly seen in the land of Israel.

This plant known as *salvia Palaestina* has one main stem in the center and three branches on each side opposite to each other. In the narrative of Exodus 25:40, Moses is instructed by God to have a lampstand of pure gold made in that shape with the admonishment to: *See that you do the design as shown to you on the mountain.*

The tree-like form of the menorah has also been associated with the Tree of Life, *Etz Hayim*, the Jewish symbol for the Torah, as a source of knowledge for one's life. The seven branches also symbolize completion and perfection like Sabbath, which completes the week. The menorah was lighted with clear oil of beaten olives.

Sabbath observance was instituted, by learning about the story of gathering the manna, and having a double portion on the sixth day in order to rest from work on the seventh day, as it is expressed in Exodus 16:22-23:

On the sixth day they gathered twice as much food, two omers each, and when the principal leaders of the community came and told Moses, he said, that was what the Lord had said. Tomorrow is a day of rest, a sabbath that is holy to the Lord. Bake what you need to bake, and boil what you need to boil, and whatever is left over put it aside to keep for the morning.

For generations scholars have questioned the nature of manna, a fine and flaky substance left after the dew evaporated. Numbers 11:7 says it resembled coriander seed.

The manna looked like coriander seed, the color of bdellium.

Fragrances and Seduction

The Bible has three botanical categories that consist of grasses, signifying all low plants, herbs including all herbaceous plants, and trees. Some are food crops, and others are mentioned for their qualities as fragrance or herbal cures.

Bdellium, a fragrant resinous tree in the Garden of Eden, is the first botanical term in Genesis, appearing in 2:12 "*…bdellium is there, and lapis lazuli...*" Frankincense from the Boswellia tree and myrrh from the Commiphora tree were also there, and both were known for their fragrance. They would be used later as incense offerings in Temple rituals.

Myrrh is first mentioned as one of the ingredients to be used with olive oil as a sacred anointing oil in the Tabernacle, as indicated in Exodus 30:22-23:

The Lord said to Moses to take five hundred shekels of myrrh, half as much, that is two hundred and fifty shekels of fragrant cinnamon…

Myrrh is also the most mentioned desirable fragrance throughout the Bible. The priest garments were perfumed with myrrh, as mentioned in Psalms 45:8:

All your garments smell like myrrh, aloes, and cassia. Out of ivory palaces stringed instruments have made you glad.

In Esther 2:12 young girls were perfumed and beautified for twelve months before they were presented to king *Ahasuerus…six months with oil of myrrh and six months with perfumes and women's cosmetics.*

In Proverbs 7:17 myrrh is also mentioned as perfume to add to the bed of a woman who wanted to seduce a man:

I have perfumed my bed with myrrh, aloes, and cinnamon.

In Solomon's writings frankincense and myrrh are part of the fragrance garden that is poetically associated with personal perfume and love.

Who is this who comes up from the wilderness like pillars of smoke, perfumed with myrrh and frankincense, with all spices of the merchant?
The Song of Songs 4:6

And written in erotic overtones:

I rose up to open for my beloved. My hands dripped with myrrh, My fingers with liquid myrrh, On the handles of the bolt.
The Song of Songs 5:5

In Genesis the sister rivalry between Leah and Rachel is associated with the mandrake, a plant linked with fertility and love.

Once, at the time of the wheat harvest, Reuben was out in the countryside, and he found some mandrakes and brought them to his mother Leah. Rachel asked Leah for some of her son's mandrakes.

But, Leah answered, "Is it not enough that you have taken my husband, but now you want these mandrakes also?" Rachel said, "In exchange for your son's mandrakes, let Jacob sleep with you tonight."
Genesis 30:14-15

The mandrake plant has a mysterious aura like no other plant in the Bible. It is mentioned in only two places: in Genesis 30:14-15, and in The Song of Songs 7:14. Mandrake is of the nightshade family, which includes poisonous plants like nightshade and jimsonweed. Its particular long root has a human-like shape. (Musselman 2007:181) Another plant associated with desire is the caper berry, whose Hebrew root *avah*, means desire. It is only mentioned once in the Bible in Ecclesiastes 12:5 *"…the caper bush may bud again…"*

The Bible mentions six types of fruit trees: fig, grape, olive, pomegranate, date, and apple, and it is abundant with poetry in which fruit trees are portrayed with metaphorical qualities. That gives us interesting insight into the inner world of thought and imagination of the biblical writers. The tree that has attracted most attention is the Tree of Knowledge of good and bad. What kind of fruit tree was it? Scholars and translators have suggested four possibilities: apple (*pyrus malus*), citron (*citrus medica*), apricot (*prunus armeniaca*), and quince (*cydonia vulgaris*).

The Apple

No other biblical plant has given rise to so much discussion about its identification as the apple tree. Biblical Hebrew does not have a specific word for apple, but both *tappuach*, meaning a fleshy fruit, and *peri*, a general term for fruit have been translated as apple. Both usages have brought dispute among botanists and linguists, who have often expressed that neither of these words should have been translated as apple.

Hebrew lexicographers associate the word *tappuach* with scent and roundness. Botanists Harold Moldenke and Alma Moldenke, in *Plants of the Bible* (1952:185) describe the *tappuach* as follows:

The apple tree of the Scriptures was a tree which afforded a pleasant shade. Its fruit was enticing to the sight, sweet to the taste, imparting fragrance, with restorative properties, and of a golden color, borne amid silvery leaves.

The word *tappuach* refers to fleshy fruits as citron, quince, fig, apricot, and other fruits similar to the apple. The citron and quince are not sweet to the taste and the wild apple, which grew in Israel, is a small, acid, woody fruit. The Moldenkes concluded that the only fruit grown in Israel that coincides with the references in the Bible is the apricot (*prunus armeniaca*). It is round and sweet of taste and fragrance. It is also the most abundant tree in the Holy Land after the fig. (Moldenke and Moldenke 1952:187)

Although the term *tappuach* is frequently used as a metaphorical reference to love, it is also used as a place name in reference to orchards.

In The Song of Songs (**Shir HaShirim**) 2:5:

Strengthen me with raisins,
refresh me with **tappuach***;*
for I am faint with love.

Also in The Song of Songs 8:5:

Who is this who comes up from the wilderness, leaning on her beloved?
Under the **tappuach** *tree I awakened you.*
There your mother conceived you.
There she was in labor and bore you.

On the other hand, the Hebrew word *peri*, which simply means "fruit", was the term used for the Garden of Eden account with Adam and Eve. Of "the fruit" (*peri*) hanging from the Tree of Knowledge of good and bad in the middle of the garden God said:

You should not eat it or touch it, or you will die…The woman looked at the tree, seeing that the **peri** *would be good to eat. It was beautiful to look at, and tempting as a source of wisdom. So, she took some and ate it, and she gave some to her husband, and he ate it.*
Genesis 3:3-6.

How did the general word for fruit in Hebrew become apple in the Christian world of Western Europe? The apple was an important image in Greek and Roman mythology and classical thought, which seems to have influenced early Christian imagery. Since the first artistic representations of the Temptation were made by Christians in Italy, the tempting fruit of the tree could easily have been understood as the apple. One of the earliest depictions of the Temptation is in the *San Gennaro* Catacombs in Naples from second century C.E., and it shows the apple as the forbidden fruit.

In the fourth century C.E. Pope Damasus ordered his leading scholar, Jerome, to translate the Bible into Latin. The result was the Vulgate Bible, based on the Latin spoken by common people.

In translating Genesis, Jerome interpreted the Hebrew word *peri* as apple, and that became a story in and of itself. In the phrase "the Tree of Knowledge of good and bad", he correctly used the Latin term *malus* for bad or evil. In a curious twist, the Latin term for apple is *malum*. In what might have been a pun too easy to resist, Jerome translated the fruit (*peri*) of the Tree of Knowledge of good and bad (*malus*) as the apple (*malum*).

The apple was the sweet fruit from his homeland, so sweet that he might have imagined it as a forbidden fruit. Until the modern day, apple has been embedded in the thought of Western Europe as the forbidden fruit, and literary works and art have repeatedly shown the apple in the story of Adam and Eve.

We find two interesting contrasting images. One is from an early Spanish document, the *codex Aemilianensis* from 994 C.E., in the library of *El Escorial*. The tree of good and bad is depicted as a fig tree with a coiled snake around it. Adam and Eve are eating figs, as well as having the fig leaf covering their "nakedness." (Jules Janick 2007) Secondly, Michelangelo's frescoes from early 1500's in the Sistine Chapel also feature the Tree of Knowledge of good and bad as a fig tree with a coiled snake around it.

But, the engraving of the German artist Albrecht Dūrer in 1504 was more widely available to the public, and it showed Adam and Eve covering themselves with apple leaves next to an apple tree with a coiled snake, and his image had the greater popular influence.

In 1667 John Milton used the apple imagery in his epic poem *Paradise Lost*, as the forbidden fruit. Milton, a renown Cambridge scholar, knowledgeable in Greek, Latin, and Hebrew interchanged the generic word "fruit", which was the correct translation of Hebrew, with specific references to apple in his poetic account of Genesis.

The first tree mentioned by name in the Garden of Eden is the fig tree when Adam and Eve used its leaves to cover their nakedness:

Then, their eyes were opened, and they realized that they were naked, so they sewed fig leaves together and made loincloths for themselves.
Genesis 3:7

Was the fig the fruit of the Tree of Knowledge from which they ate? Babylonian Talmudic scholars think so, and rabbinical commentators have frequently mentioned the fig as the possibility for the Tree of Knowledge.

Social and Symbolic Significance

In Hebrew we find social and symbolic significance to fruits in reference to people and cities, laws, proverbs and traditions. For example, Aaron's priestly garments were decorated with pomegranates:

On its hem make pomegranates of blue, purple and crimson with golden bells between them the whole way around...
Exodus 28:33.

Images of fruits are also used as decoration on the walls of Solomon's Temple as it is written in 1 Kings 6:29-32:

He carved figures of cherubim, palm trees, and flowers on all of the walls of the house, both inside and outside...The doors were made of olive wood, and he carved cherubim, palms, and flowers on them, overlaying them with gold, hammering the gold onto the cherubim and the palms.

There are laws about how to gather and share specific fruits. We read in Deuteronomy 24:20-22:

Garden of Eden

When you beat your olive trees for fruit, do not take everything. What is left is for the foreigner, the fatherless and the widow...When you gather grapes from your vineyard, do not pick them a second time; leave something for the foreigner, the fatherless, and the widow. Remember that you were forced laborers in Egypt, and that is why I give this commandment to you.

Fruits are used as metaphors and blessings or curses, and as teaching tools in Proverbs. In Hosea we find contrasting metaphors for Israel in 9:10:

*I found Israel like grapes in the wilderness.
Your fathers are like the first ripening of the fig tree;
But they came to Baal Peor, and turned to shamefulness
And they became as detested as they had been loved.*

And in contrast in Hosea 10:1 we read:

Israel is like a rich vine that produces its fruit. When the fruit was abundant, he multiplied his altars. When the land prospered, the cultic altars abounded.

We read of the seven special crops of the land, and blessings to the Israelites. In Deuteronomy 8:7-8, Moses refers to the abundance in the promised land of Canaan:

The Lord your God is bringing you into a good land, one with streams, springs, and fountains in the hills and in the plain. It is a land of wheat and barley, of vines, figs, and pomegranates with olive trees, and honey.

We also read of curses using fruit as metaphor in Deuteronomy 28:40:

You will have olive trees throughout your territory, but you should not anoint yourselves with the oil or the olives will drop off.

The Five Most Mentioned Fruits in the Hebrew Bible

Fig Tree

Whoever tends the fig tree will enjoy its fruit.
He who looks after his master will be honored.
Proverbs 27:18

The fig is one of the oldest known fruit trees and the Hebrew word for fig, *te'enah*, is not found originally in any other Semitic language, which suggests that the tree is perhaps indigenous to the territory of the Israelites. In the archaeological excavations of *Gezer*, a famous biblical city in Judea, remnants of figs were found dating back to the Neolithic about 5,000 B.C.E. (Goor 1965:124ff)

The fig and vine are often paired in the Bible for they were frequently planted side by side with the vine climbing up the fig tree. Figs provided year round nourishment whether fresh or dried, squeezed together into a cake or bread, and people lived on dried figs when they traveled long distances. Figs were used medicinally, and its wood was used as fuel in cooking. In Numbers 13:23 when Moses sent spies to check the land they brought back "*pomegranates and figs*". The fig is mentioned repeatedly as food, as in I Samuel 25:18:

Abigail quickly gathered two hundred loaves of bread...a hundred bunches of raisins and two hundred cakes of dried figs and loaded them on donkeys.

And in I Samuel 30:11-12

They encountered an Egyptian in open country and took him to David. They gave him food to eat and water to drink and some dried figs and two bunches of raisins. After eating he regained strength...

The Prophets warned the Israelites that if they would not walk on the path of righteousness (wisdom) the fig would vanish, and if they were devout the fig would yield its fruit.

I will lay waste her vines and her fig trees, about which she has said, "These are my wages that my lovers have given me."
I will make them into brush that the animals of the field will eat.
Hosea 2:12

Figs are also mentioned as having medicinal properties, in Isaiah 38:21 it reads:

Let them take a cake of figs and apply it to the rash, and he will recover.

The shade of the fig tree and the grapevine are metaphors for peace, happiness security, wealth and plenty. In Mica 4:4 we read:

But every man will sit under his grapevine or fig tree.
No one will make them afraid,
Because the Lord of hosts has spoken.

In I Kings 4:25 we read:

Throughout Solomon's reign the people of Judah and Israel lived in peace, everyone from Dan to Beersheba under his own vine and his own fig tree.

The ripen fig was beloved, it was good to eat and gave nourishment, but the rotten fig was an image of bitterness and evil. Jeremiah talks about the properties of the fig and metaphorically distinguishes between the good and evil in people. Jeremiah told the people to submit to king *Nebuchadnezzar*, the Babylonian king who had conquered their land. If they did, they would be blessed; if not, disaster would come upon them. Two baskets of figs, one good and one bad, were set in front of the temple to represent the two groups of Jews.

Then the Lord said to me, "What do you see, Jeremiah?" I said, "Figs. The good ones are very good, and the bad ones are very bad, so bad that they cannot be eaten."...The Lord, the God of Israel said: "Like these good figs, so I will treat the exiles from Judah...And like the bad figs, that cannot be eaten, because they are so bad," said the Lord, "So I will treat Zedekiah the king of Judah...I will...make them a taunt and a curse...
Jeremiah 24:3-9

In biblical times the fig was sanctified and brought to the temple as a gift. It was a fruit with a high rank among the fruits of the Land, and unlike many other fruits it was eaten entirely as it is, skin, pulp and seeds. In the Babylonian Talmud the words of the Torah were likened to a fig tree because the more you searched for fruit the more you found it, and in Torah, the more you study the more wisdom you find.

Grapevine

I found Israel as enjoyable as grapes in the wilderness.
Hosea 9:10

The earliest evidence of grape seeds was found in excavations in Jericho, dating 3000 B.C.E. In the Bible and in other early Hebrew writings the grape is the most mentioned fruit (*gefen*) in all its forms, as grapes, wine, raisins, syrup and vinegar, and its cultivation is a symbol of bounty and of God's blessings. Genesis refers to a vineyard planted by Noah in the mountain of Ararat as the first plant grown after the flood.

Noah, who was the first to till the soil, planted a vineyard. He drank the wine and became drunk and lay undressed in his tent.
Genesis 9:20-21

Offering wine was a courtesy, as we see when Abraham met with King Melchizedek of Salem (Jerusalem).

Melchizedek, the king of Salem, brought bread and wine. He was a priest of God Most High.
Genesis 14:18

Vineyards were commonly hedged with walls of fieldstones, and their flowers were described as fragrant in King Solomon's poems:

The vines are in blossom and give out their fragrance. Arise, my love, my beautiful one, and come away.
The Song of Songs 2:13

In Genesis 49:11-12 we read some of the uses of grapes and the grapevine:

*He ties his donkey to a vine,
and its colt to the choice vine.
He washes his clothing in wine,
His robe in the blood of grapes.*

The grape and wine are mentioned hundreds of times in the Bible. Wine was an economic asset used widely in ancient Israel. Red wine was commonly used to dye cloths, and wine was mixed with water as a purifier. It was used medicinally for intestinal ailments and mixed with oil to rub the sick. When it was added to barley, it fermented as vinegar for food. In Ruth 2:14 Boaz says to Ruth:

*Come over here and partake of the meal,
and deep your morsel in the vinegar.*

And in Proverbs 10:26 vinegar is mentioned as a metaphor for discomfort or problem:

Like vinegar to the teeth, and smoke to the eyes, so is the lazy man to those who send him to do a task.

All regions of Israel had grapes. It is written that king David had stewards exclusively for his vineyards and wine cellars as we read in I Chronicles 27:26-27:

Ezri the son of Chelub was over those who did the agricultural work. Shimei from Ramah was over the vineyards. Zabdi of Shephem was over the increase of the vineyards for the wine cellars.

Vineyards, are a metaphor for success, a symbol of reward and God's blessing throughout the Bible. In Jeremiah 31:5-12 we read:

*Again you will plant vineyards on the hills of Samaria. The planters will plant fruit and enjoy it... They will come and sing on the heights of Zion,
and will flow to the bounty of the Lord, to the grain, to the new wine, to the oil...
Their soul will be as a watered garden.
They will not sorrow any more at all.*

In Genesis, Joseph grew up familiar with vineyards, and he was competent in interpreting dreams relating to the vine for the Pharaoh's cupbearer:

In my dream, there was a vine in front of me. The vine had three branches. As soon as it had budded, it blossomed, and its clusters ripened into grapes.
Genesis 40:9-10

When Moses sent the scouts to check on the land, they came back with oversized cultivated grapes slung on a pole:

They came to the wadi Eshcol, where they cut a branch with a single bunch of grapes, and it had to be carried on a pole by two men, and they gathered pomegranates and figs.
Numbers 13:23.

At the end of the Exodus from Egypt the Israelites entered the Promised Land where they found many vineyards and were blessed with the seven species (wheat, barley, vines, figs, pomegranates, olives, and dates) mentioned in Deuteronomy 8:7-8.

The culture of grapes and the technology of wine making are common themes in biblical writings and religious practices. There are many place-names linked with the vine and wine, such as *Beit Hakerem*, (house of the vineyard) in Jeremiah 6:1, *Nahal Eshcol* (brook of the cluster) in Numbers 13:23, *Enav* (grape) near *Hebron* in Joshua 11:21.

The vine was associated with blessings and joy in Isaiah 5:1-2

My beloved had a vineyard high on a fertile hill. He prepared the land, cleared it of stones, and planted it with the best vines. He built a watchtower in the middle; he carved out a wine vat. He expected it to yield the best grapes.

At the end of the Exodus from Egypt, when the Israelites entered the Promised Land, they found many vineyards:

…vineyards and olive groves that you did not plant…you will have all you want to eat. Don't forget the Lord who brought you out of the land of Egypt, out of the land of bondage.
 Deuteronomy 6:11-12.

We can glean technical details about pruning of the vine as in Isaiah 18:5

After the budding is complete, when the blossoms ripen into berries, he will cut the shoots with pruning knives and cut and clear excess branches.

 And we read about irrigation of the vine in Isaiah 27:2-3:

On that day, sing about the delightful vineyard, I, the Lord, keep watch over it and water it regularly so that its leaves do not wilt. I keep watch over it day and night.

The vine is a symbol of prosperity and plenty and the Prophet Ezekiel compared the well-being of the people of Israel to the luxuriance of the vine:

It grew and became a spreading vine of low stature, with leafy branches that turned toward him, and its roots stayed under him.
Ezekiel 17:6

The grape has such importance in biblical narration that it has been said that a vineyard is like the richness of the whole world.

Olive

The dove came back to him towards evening with a freshly plucked olive leaf in its beak, and Noah knew that the water had subsided from the surface of the earth.
Genesis 8:11

The Hebrew word for olive is *zayit*, which some suggest is related to the noun *ziv*, luminescence, making reference to the silvery beauty of the underside of its leaves and to its unique glimmering shine as an oil, distinct from other oils.

The olive and the grape are the most mentioned fruits in the Bible. Archaeological evidence of the olive tree dates to 10,000 B.C.E., and it was the most important fruit tree for the ancient Israelites. (Goor 1966:223ff)

The olive tree gave oil that was used to burn as light, cook, and even to apply to the skin. Psalms 104:15 says, "oil that makes the face shine". Olive oil was also used for medicine, and it was an important commercial crop. Olive orchards were important location landmarks, and they were used to name places, such as *Kerem Zayit* (olive grove), in Judges 15:5, or *Bar Zayit* (olive forest) in I Chronicles: 7. The olive became a symbol of beauty, fertility, freshness, wealth, fame, wisdom, and peace.

The first biblical mention of the olive is in Genesis 8:11 in the story of the flood when the dove came back to Noah with an olive leaf in its beak. In other biblical references the grape vine and the olive tree are metaphorically linked to happiness and prosperity, as in Psalms 128:1-3.

You will be happy, and it will be well with you. Your wife will be like a fruitful vine within your house, and your sons sitting around your table will be like olive saplings.

The olive was also a symbol of purity, clarity, strength and abundance. Olive oil is a protagonist in many biblical passages. Olives were brought as offerings to the temple, and they were cited as the mainstay of the table of poor as well as rich.

In Jeremiah 11:16 Israel was called an olive tree: *The Lord gave your name, "A green olive tree, beautiful with goodly fruit."*

The first pressing of the purest oil was used to light the Temple Menorah.

Order the Israelites to bring pure oil of beaten olives ready for the regular lighting of the lamps.
Exodus 27:20.

Olive oil was also used to anoint kings and priests, to treat the sick, light homes, and for cosmetics and perfumes. Judges 9:8-11 says:

Once the trees set out to anoint a king over themselves. They said to the olive tree, "Be king over us." But the olive tree answered, "Would I abandon my rich oil, honored by God and men, to go and rule over the trees?"

The secret of the longevity of the olive tree is its remarkable expanded root system and durability, which was used as a metaphor for the virtues of righteousness and constancy:

But I am like a green olive tree in God's house. I trust in God's loving kindness forever and ever.
Psalms 52:10

Olive oil, wheat and wine were the staples of life to be stockpiled against the day of enemy action as is cited in 2 Chronicles 11:11:

He strengthened the defenses of the fortified towns and named governors over them with stores of food, oil and wine.

In the narrative of Joel we read in 2:24:

The threshing floors will be full of wheat, and the vats will overflow with new wine and oil.

When the Israelites conquered Canaan the olive tree was among their blessings.

The Lord your God will bring you into the land...with houses full of good...vineyards and olive groves that you did not plant...you will have all you want to eat.
Deuteronomy 6:10-11

We read in Joshua verse 24:13:

I have given you land which you had not worked and towns which you had not built, and you have settled in them. You are enjoying the vineyards and olive groves that you did not plant.

The olive tree was in every region and the narrative mentions how King David had overseers for the royal olive trees and oil stocks:

Baal Hanan the Gederite supervised the olive trees and the sycamore trees that were in the lowland. Joash was in charge of the cellars of oil.
I Chronicles 27:28

The olive was an important food and there was a commandment not to withhold it from any one and not to harvest it in completeness, but to leave for the gleaners.

When you beat your olive trees for fruit, do not take everything. What is left is for the foreigner, the fatherless and the widow...

When you gather grapes from your vineyard, do not pick them a second time; leave something for the foreigner, the fatherless, and the widow. Remember that you were forced laborers in Egypt, and that is why I give this commandment to you.
Deuteronomy 24:20-22

There is also a curse referring to olives in Deuteronomy 28:40.

You will have olive trees throughout your territory, but you should not anoint yourselves with the oil or the olives will drop off.

The Prophets metaphorically teach about the value of the olive tree.

*His branches will spread out,
and his beauty will be like the olive tree.*
Hosea 14:7

In the narrative of Prophets there is the vision of Zecharia about the gold candelabrum and two olive trees one on each side.

...have seen a golden lampstand with a bowl above. There are seven lamps on it, and there are seven pipes to each of the lamps. There are two olive trees, one on the right side of the bowl, and the other on the left side of it.
Zecharia 4:2-3.

Olive oil in Jewish symbolism stood for peace and well-being, for happiness, vigor, fertility, joy of living and wisdom.

Date Palm

The righteous shall flourish like the date palm.
Psalm 92:13

The date palm has existed in the Jordan River basin since the Neolithic age (6000-4000 B.C.E.). It also existed in the coastal areas from Phoenicia (modern day Lebanon) to Acre in northern Israel. The word "phoenix" was the name of the date in early Greek, suggesting the connection with Phoenicia. (Goor 1967:320ff) The scientific name of the date palm is *Phoenix dactylifera*, and in Hebrew the word is *tamar* or *tomer*. (Jensen 2012)

For Israelites, the date was a symbol of sanctity. At the feast of Tabernacles (*Sukkot*), they would say a blessing over it and decorate the Sukkah huts with palm leaves:

On the first day take the fruit of the citrus trees, palm-fonds, the branches of leafy trees and willows by the creek, and rejoice before the Lord your God for seven days.
Leviticus 23:40.

On *sukkot* the four species-citron, palm, myrtle, and willow continue to be blessed to this day. Palm leaves stood for harmony and peace and any important or sacred building would have them.

He carved figures of cherubim, palm trees, and flowers on all of the walls of the house, both inside and outside...The doors were made of olive wood, and he carved cherubim, palms, and flowers on them, overlaying them with gold, hammering the gold onto the cherubim and the palms.
I Kings 6:29-32.

In Deuteronomy 34:3, Jericho is mentioned as the city of date palm,

The Negeb; and the plain-the Valley of Jericho, the city of palm trees-as far as Zoar.

Date-pits have been discovered archaeologically around Jericho dating from approximately 1,600 B.C.E. (Goor 1967:320ff).

The first mention of the date palm in the Bible is in Exodus when the Israelites led by Moses departed from Egypt. In a matter of days, they arrived to the oasis of Elim (Exodus 15:27) that had twelve springs and seventy date palms (*tamarim*). The mention of seventy date palms suggests the mystical determinant of plentitude.

They arrived to Elim where there were twelve springs and seventy palm trees, and they camped there next to the water.

In the Bible the date palm is regarded as a status symbol of being righteous and honorable and of having grace and beauty. Song of Songs 7:6-7 says:

How beautiful you are, so entrancing.
My beloved, daughter of delights?
Your stately form is like a palm tree,
your breasts like its clusters of fruit.

In Psalms the righteous are metaphorically compared to a date palm, in Psalm 1:3,

He will be like a tree planted by the
streams of water,
that produces its fruit in its season,
whose foliage does not wither.
Whatever it produces will thrive.

In Psalm 92:13-14 *The righteous shall flourish like the palm tree.*

Names suggestive of the date, *Tamar*, are popular in the Bible as a name for women: *Judah got a wife for Er his first-born, her name was Tamar.* Genesis 38:6. *Tamar* was also the name of king David's daughter and half sister of his son *Amnon* who said to the king

Let my sister Tamar come and make
breadcakes in front of me and serve them
to me herself.
2 Samuel 13:6

There are geographical places named for dates like *Baal-tamar,* a date palm sanctuary.

Genesis 14:7 says: *...and also the Amorites who dwelt in Hazazon-tamar*, meaning the place where many clusters of dates were cut and gathered from the palm trees. In 2 Chronicles 20:2 *Hazazon-tamar* is identified with *Ein-Gedi*, Ezekiel 47:19 mentions a *Tamar* in the Negev:

The southern boundary shall be from
Tamar as far as the waters of Meriboth
Kadesh along the Wadi to the great sea.
That is the boundary.

In the biblical period Egypt had date palms, but they were interested in the quality and varieties of the dates coming from the Valley of the Jordan. A wall painting in Karnak from 1500 B.C.E. shows those palms along with other plants brought back to Egypt by a pharaoh who had conquered the region. (Goor 1967:320ff).

It is said that the date has its roots in the water and its crest in the sun, a poetical allusion to its need for water and abundant sun to ripen this fruit that produces honey. The Oasis of Sinai had similar conditions as Egypt, Mesopotamia, and the Jordan Rift Valley for the cultivation of date palms.

The tree had countless uses; its fruit was sweet whether fresh or dried, it was available in all seasons, its branches were used for building and for celebrations. Date palm trees can live for hundreds of years, and they symbolize life. It was considered by some as the Tree of Life, because even after fire it sends up new shoots.

Pomegranate

I would have you drink spiced wine,
of the juice of my pomegranate.
The Song of Songs 8:2

Pomegranate, *Rimmon*, in Hebrew, was cultivated in the Land more than 5,000 years ago. After the Israelites reached Canaan under Joshua and began farming the land, they spread the cultivation of pomegranates throughout the area. In ancient Egypt pomegranates were imported as well as raisins, olives and figs from nearby Canaan, the pomegranate import was depicted in the wall decorations of the "Botanical Chamber" in Karnak (1504-1450 BCE) (Jensen 2012)

When the Israelites went to scout the land from the wilderness of *Zion*:

They came to the wadi Eshcol, where they cut a branch with a single bunch of grapes, and it had to be carried on a pole by two men, and they gathered pomegranates and figs.
Numbers 13:23

Pomegranate for the Israelites and Canaanites was the symbol of beauty, plenty, and fertility due to the beauty of its flower, and the multitude of seeds that the fruit has. It was an element of adornment in buildings and on garments and ornaments of daily use. In fact, the pomegranate's calyx served as model for Solomon's royal crown. The crown on the Torah and the regalia of Jewish priests were hemmed with an embroidery of pomegranates alternating with bells of pure gold:

On its hem make pomegranates of blue, purple and crimson with golden bells between them all the way around; a golden bell and a pomegranate all the way around the hem of the garment.
Exodus 28:33-34.

Pomegranate images were cast by the artist Hiram on the Temple's columns

He made the columns with two rows of pomegranates around the top of the ornamental pattern of one column, and he did the same on the other capital.
1 Kings 7:18.

When the children of Israel were taken into captivity, the pomegranates on the pillars are specifically mentioned in Jeremiah 52:17-23

The Chaldeans broke the pillars of bronze that were in the House of the Lord…There were ninety-six pomegranates on the sides. There were one hundred on the meshwork all around.

There are a plethora of place names for *Rimmon* in the Bible. In Numbers 33:19: "they set out from Rithmah and encamped at Rimmon–parez", in Judges 20:47:

The six hundred men who survived fled into the wilderness to the Rock of Rimmon where they stayed for four months.

Reference to the rimmon appears in Joshua 15:32 and 19:7, in Nehemiah 11:29: *Ein Rimmon* (Spring of the Pomegranate). In 2 Kings 6:18:

…when I bow low in the temple of Rimmon, may the LORD pardon your servant in this.

The pomegranate tree was a shade offering tree for monarchs and their subjects in 1 Samuel 14:2 we read:

Now Saul was staying on the outskirts of Gibeah, under the pomegranate tree at Migron, and the troops with him numbered about 600.

The beauty and splendor of the green pomegranate shrub, and the red and pink color of the flower and fruit with its ruby like seeds inside symbolized beauty, sanctity, fertility and abundance.

In the poetry of The Song of Songs the pomegranate is a metaphor for beauty.

… Your brow is like a piece of a pomegranate behind your veil.
The Song of Songs 4:3

*Your shoots are an orchard of pomegranates, with all precious fruits,
Of henna with spikenard plants,*
The Song of Songs 4:13

*Let's see whether the vine has budded,
If its blossoms have opened,
If the pomegranates are in flower.
There I will give you my love.*
The Song of Songs 7:13

In the biblical text, the pomegranate was grouped with olive, vine and fig as fruits of plenty, and all were considered worthy offerings to the Temple.

Of all the biblical fruits perhaps the most beautiful is the pomegranate, and its image was used in the garment of the High Priest, in the temple as decoration, and the calix as the crown of *Torah* and the crown of King Solomon.

The portrayal of plants in the Hebrew Bible such as the depiction of the Garden of Eden, re-enforces the lessons of ethical monotheism. The text expresses the essence of Jewish faith in the God of history Who brought forth the children of Israel from Egypt and made a covenant with them at *Sinai* to obey His laws.

If you observe the commandments that I give you on this day to love the Lord your God and serve Him with all your heart and soul, then I will send the rain for your land at the right season, both the Spring and Autumn rain, and you will gather your new grain, wine, and oil. I will give grass in the fields for your cattle, and you will have all you want to eat. Take care to not be tempted away to serve and worship other gods.
Deuteronomy 11:13-16

The concepts of "Garden of Eden" and "Paradise" have become synonymous with a fruitful comforting, delightful, and beautiful oasis of orderly design, where fruit trees, cereals, legumes, vegetables, balsams and resins, forest trees and bushes, bitter, poison and wild plants inhabit the rich lands of the Hebrew Bible.

Other Plants in the Hebrew Bible

God said,
"Look, I am giving you every plant that has seeds in all the earth and every tree that gives seed-bearing fruits. They will be yours for food..."

Genesis 1:29

*M*ake *the upright frame of the Tabernacle of acacia wood.*

EXODUS 26:15

I will plant cedars in the wilderness and acacia, myrtle, and oil trees. I will put cypress trees...in the desert.

ISAIAH 41:19

Acacia albida
Acacia
שטים

*T**he next day*
when Moses entered the Tent of Meeting,
he found that Aaron's staff, the staff of the tribe of Levi,
had budded, blossomed and produced almonds.

NUMBERS 17:23

Pterocarpus santalinus
Almug
אלמוג

*T*he king
used the wood to make decorations
for the House of the LORD and for
the palace, as well as harps and
lyres for the musicians.
Such quantities of almug wood
and precious stones have not been
imported or seen again
since that time.

1 KINGS 10:12

Like
long palm groves,
Like gardens
along a river,
Like aloe trees
planted by the Lord.

Numbers 24:6

All
your garments smell
like myrrh, aloes,
and cassia.
From ivory palaces stringed
instruments
have made you glad.

Psalms 45:9

Pyrus malus
Apple

תפוח
Tappuach

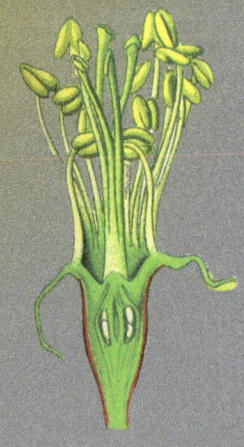

As
the apple tree is among the
trees of the wood, so is my beloved
among young men. I sat down under his
shadow with great delight,
his fruit was sweet to my taste.

The Song of Songs 2:3

*S*ustain me
with raisins,
revive me with apricots
for I am lovesick.

THE SONG OF SONGS 2:5

After they sat down to eat, they looked up and saw a caravan of Ishmaelites coming from Gilead on their way to Egypt. Their camels were carrying gum, balm, and myrrh.

GENESIS 37:25

The LORD your GOD
is bringing you to a good land
with streams, springs, and water
gushing out of the valleys and hills;
a land of wheat and barley, vines,
fig trees, and pomegranates;
a land of olive oil and dates.

DEUTERONOMY 8:7-8

Hordeum sativum
Barley
שעורה

The gold
of that land is good,
bdellium is there...

GENESIS 2:12

The manna
looked like coriander seed,
the color of bdellium.

NUMBERS 11:7

Commiphora
Bdellium
בדלח

Vicia faba
Bean
פול

Lycium

Boxthorn

אטד

*T*hen
all the trees said
to the thorn bush,
"Will you come and be king
over us?"

Judges 9:14

*T*horns
and snares are
in the path of the
wicked;
whoever takes care
of himself stays away
from them.

Proverbs 22:5

Black cumin is beaten with a stick and cumin with a rod.

ISAIAH 28:27

Nigella sativa

Black cumin

קצח

Rubus sanguineus
Bramble
סנה

An Angel
of the L ORD
appeared to him like a fire
burning out of a bush.
The bush was on fire,
but it was not
burned up.

E XODUS 3:2

May
the bounty of the land and its
fullness, with the Presence of
the One in the burning bush,
rest on the head of Joseph,
who was prince
among his brothers.

D EUTERONOMY 33:16

He laid down
under a bush, and while
he slept an angel touched
him and said,
"Get up and eat." He
looked and there beside
his head was a cake
baked on hot stones with
a jar of water.
He ate and drank and
laid down again.

1 Kings 19:5-6

Cymbopogon martini
Aromatic cane
קנה־בשם

The Lord

spoke to Moses, saying:

Next take choice spices: ...

fragrant cinnamon...aromatic cane...

and a hin of olive oil.

Make of this a sacred

anointing oil...

Exodus 30:22-25

Saccharum biflorum
Cane biflorate
אגמון

***S**o, on one day*
the L<small>ORD</small> *cut off head and*
tail, palm frond and reed from
Israel.

I<small>SAIAH</small> **9:13**

*T**he almond tree
may blossom,
and the grasshopper
will be a burden,
and the caper bush
may bud again...*

Ecclesiastes 12:5

Caparis spinosa
Caper
אביונה

The Lord God
provided a ricinus plant that grew up
over Jonah, making a shade over his
head easing his discomfort. Jonah was
happy because of the plant.

Jonah 4:6

Ricinus communis
Castor oil plant
קיקיון

Cedrus libani
Cedar
עץ ארז

*F*or all the cedars
of Lebanon,
tall and lofty
And all the oaks of Bashan

Isaiah 2:13

I destroyed
the Amorite,
whose height was like that
of cedars, and he was
stout like an oak.
I destroyed
his branches above,
and his trunk below.

Amos 2:9

*T*he oxen
and donkeys that till
the land will be fed
with seasoned fodder
that has been winnowed
with fork and shovel.

Isaiah 30:24

Cicer arietnum
Chick-pea
חמיץ

I have perfumed my bed with myrrh, aloes, and cinnamon.

PROVERBS 7:17

*O*n the first day
*take the fruit of the citrus trees, palm-fonds, the branches of leafy trees and willows by the creek, and rejoice before the L*ORD *your* G*OD for seven days.*

LEVITICUS 23:40

Israel called it manna.
It was like a white
coriander seed,
and it tasted like a wafer
made with honey.

EXODUS 16:31

The manna
looked like
coriander seed,
the color of bdellium.

NUMBERS 11:7

There were hangings of white and blue material, fastened with cords of fine linen and purple to silver rings and marble pillars. The couches were of gold and silver on a mosaic pavement of marble, mother-of-pearl, and malachite.

ESTHER 1:6

Gossypium herbraceum

Cotton

כרפס

Citrullus colocynthis
Cucumber
פקועות

The *daughter of Zion is left like a cottage in a vineyard, like a hut in a cucumber field.*

Isaiah 1:8

> **A**fter he has prepared the land, doesn't he broadcast dill and scatter cumin seeds? Doesn't he sow wheat and barley in rows and emmer along the side?
>
> **Isaiah 28:25**

Cuminum cyminum
Cumin
כמון

I will plant cedars in the wilderness and acacia, myrtle, and oil trees. I will put cypress trees...in the desert.

ISAIAH 41:19

Cupressus sempervirens

Cypress
ברוש

*L*et the wilderness and the desert be glad; let the desert rejoice and burst into flowers.

Isaiah 35:1

I am a rose of Sharon,
a lily of the valleys.
As a lily among thorns,
so is my love among the daughters.

The Song of Songs 2:1-2

She sat
under the palm tree of Deborah

JUDGES 4:5

Phoenix dactylifera

Date palm

התמר

*T*ake for yourself
also wheat, barley, beans, lentils,
millet, and spelt; combine them
in one vessel and bake them into
bread.

Ezekiel 4:9

*T*he people of Dedan traded with you. Many coasts traded under your hegemony, and they brought you ivory tusks and ebony in tribute.

EZEKIEL 27:15

Diospyros ebenum
Ebony
הבנים

Triticum dicoccum
Emmer
כסמת

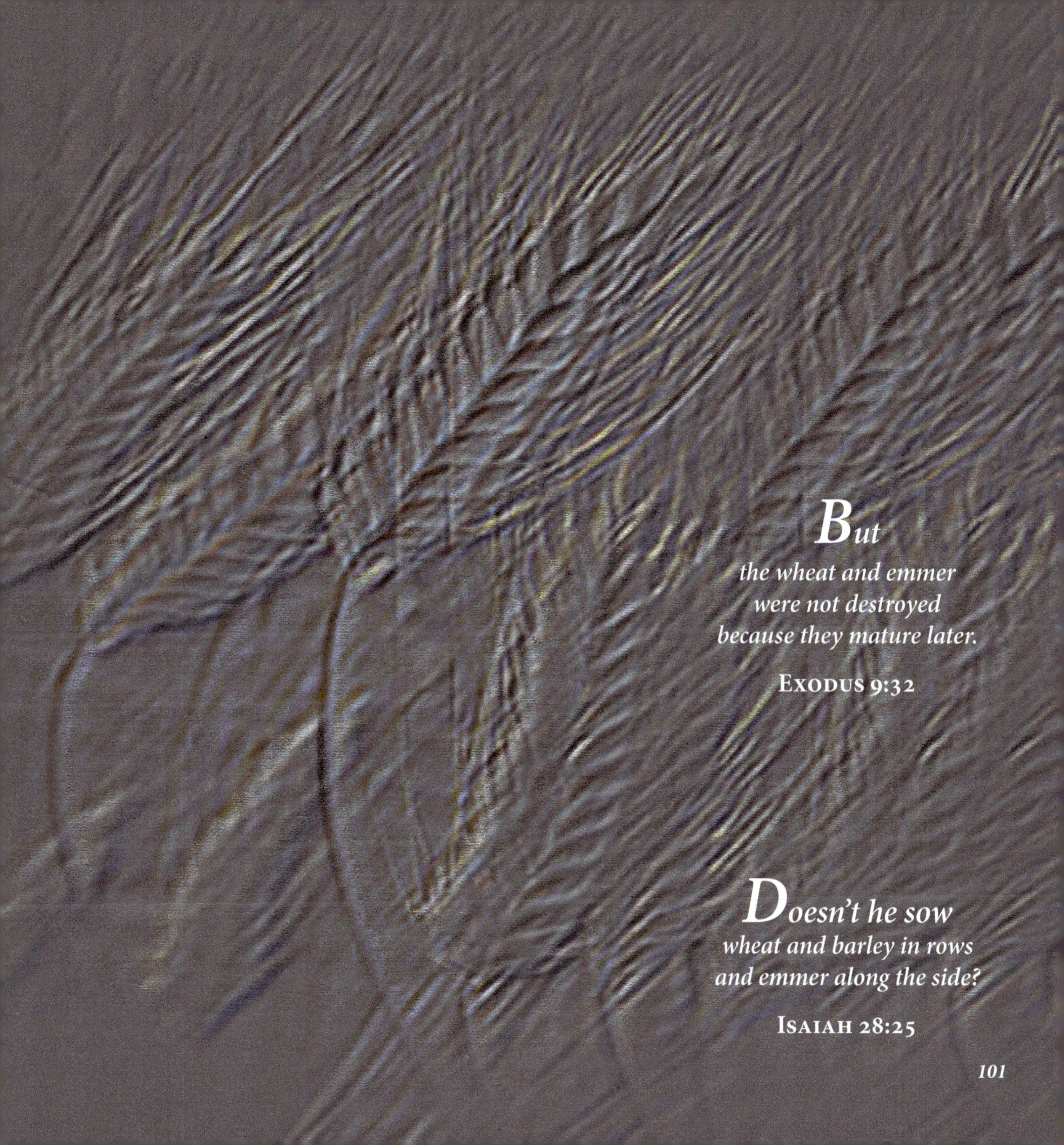

But
the wheat and emmer
were not destroyed
because they mature later.

Exodus 9:32

Doesn't he sow
wheat and barley in rows
and emmer along the side?

Isaiah 28:25

Ficus carica
Fig tree
עץ תאנה

The green figs
*ripen on the fig trees,
the vine blossoms give their fragrance,
Arise my darling,
my fair one, come away.*

THE SONG OF SONGS 2:13

They have laid
*waste to my vines,
and broken my fig trees.*

JOEL 1:7

He
made silver as common in Jerusalem as stone, and cedar as plentiful as the sycamore is in the Shephelah.

1 Kings 10:27

The bricks have fallen,
but we will rebuild with finished stone. The sycamores have been cut, but we will grow cedars in their place.

Isaiah 9:9

Ficus sycomorus

Fig sycamore

שקמה

*T*he *flax and barley were ruined because the barley was ripe and the flax was budding.*

EXODUS 9:31

*P*haraoh *took off his signet ring and put it on Joseph's finger, and he had him dressed in vestments of good linen and hung a gold chain around his neck.*

GENESIS 41:42

And the LORD said to Moses, take fragrant spices, gum resin, aromatic shell, galbanum with pure frankincense together with the spices in equal parts. Blend it as a pure, sacred incense by the incense-maker's craft.

EXODUS 30:34-35

We remember *the fish that we used to eat free in Egypt, the cucumbers, the melons, the leeks, the onions, and the garlic.*

NUMBERS 11:5

Allium sativum

Garlic

שום

> *The cedar inside the house had carvings of gourds and flowers. It was all cedar, no stone was visible.*
>
> 1 KINGS 6:18

Legenaia vulgaris
Gourd
דלעת

113

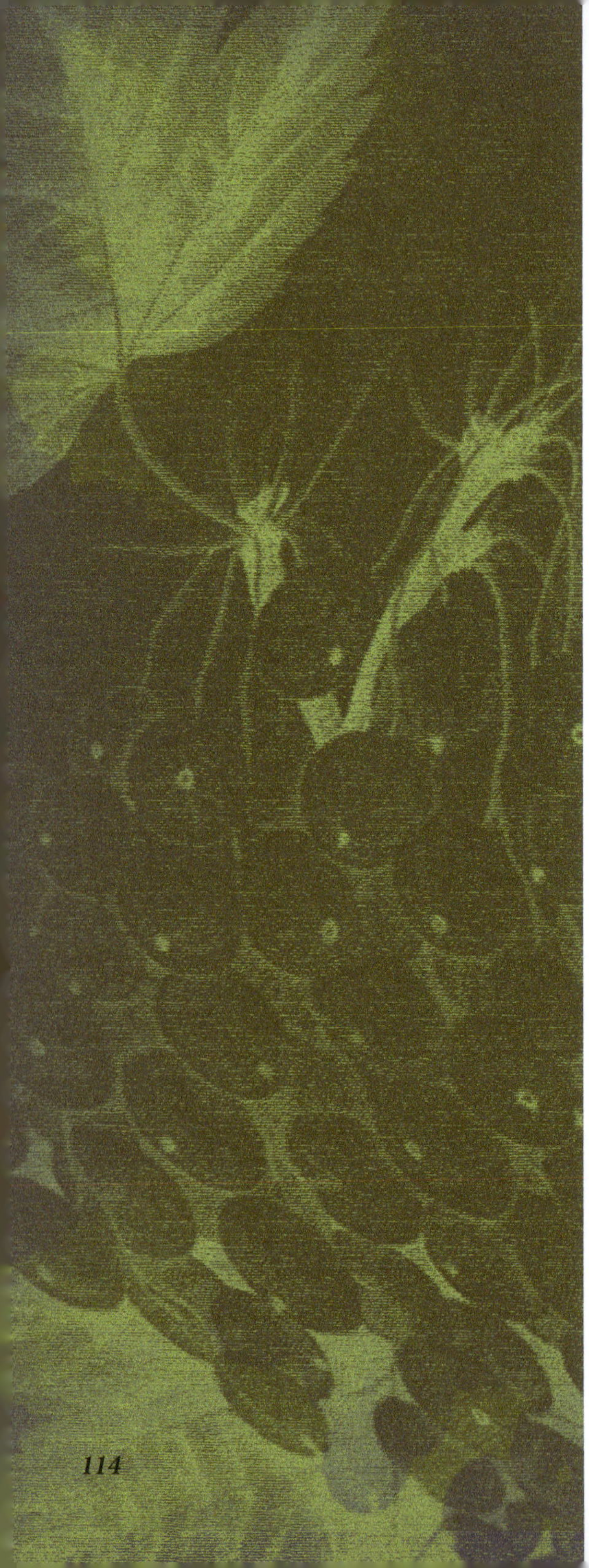

When you go
into another man's vineyard,
you may eat as many grapes
as you wish until you are full.
But, you must not put any in
your basket.

Deuteronomy 23:25

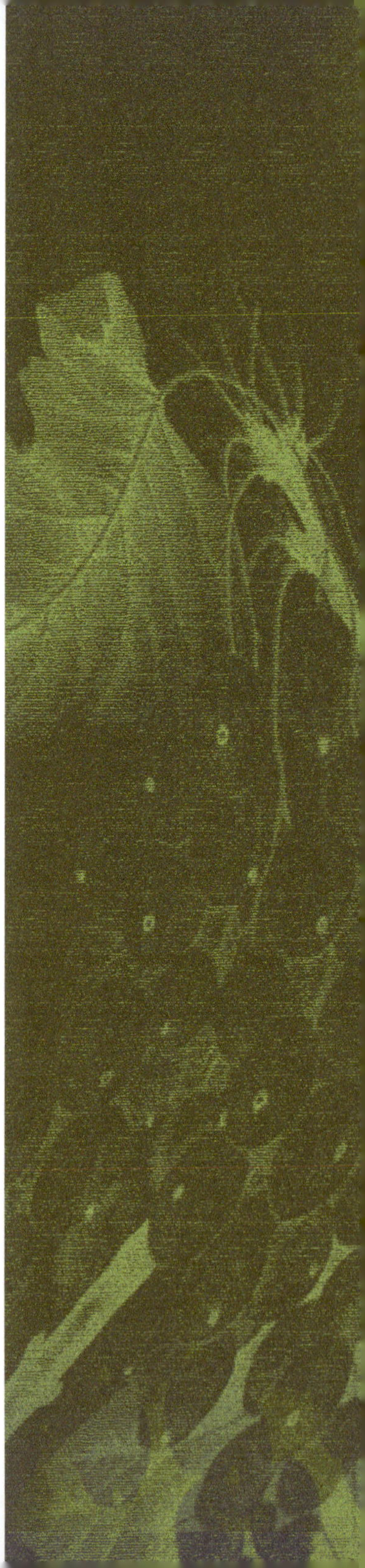

My beloved is to me
a cluster of henna blossoms
from the vineyards of En Gedi.

THE SONG OF SONGS 1:14

Your shoots are an orchard
of pomegranates, with all precious fruits,
henna with spikenard plants.

THE SONG OF SONGS 4:13

Purify me with hyssop
until I am clean.
Wash me until I am whiter than
snow.

Psalms 51:9

Taking a bunch
of hyssop, dip it in blood in a
basin and put the blood from
the basin on the lintel and the
two doorposts. No one should
go out of the door of the house
until morning.

Exodus 12:22

Zizyphus spina

Jujube
צאלים

He lies
under the lotus trees,
under the cover of the reed,
and the marsh.
The lotuses cover him
with their shade.
The willows of the brook
surround him.

JOB 40:21-22

> **T**he pines and cedars of Lebanon shout, "Since you have been knocked down, no one has come to cut us down."
>
> **ISAIAH 14:8**

Juniperus exelsa
Juniper
ברוש

Cistus ladanum
Ladanum
לט

Put in your baggage some of the best products of the land as a gift for the man, some balm and honey, gum tragacanth, myrrh, pistachio nuts, and almonds.

Genesis 43:11

Laurus Nobilis
Laurel
אֶרֶן

I saw a wicked man in great power who spread himself like a green laurel tree.

Psalms 37:35

We remember that in Egypt we could easily eat fish, cucumbers, melons, leeks, onions and garlic.

Numbers 11:5

Then,
*Jacob gave Esau bread
and lentil stew,
and he ate and drank
and went his way.
That is how Esau
repudiated his birthright.*

Genesis 25:34

The Philistines
*had gathered
where there was a field
with a good crop of lentils,
and the people fled
from the Philistines.*

2 Samuel 23:11

Lens esculenta
Lentils
עדשים

*My beloved
has gone down to his garden,
To the beds of spices,
To delight in the gardens
And to gather lilies.*

THE SONG OF SONGS 6:2

Lilium madonna

Lilies

שושנים

Mandragora officinarum
Mandrake
דודא

*W*hen the mandrakes give their perfume, all choice fruits are at our door, from the newly picked to the long stored. I have kept them for you, my beloved.

THE SONG OF SONGS 7:14

*M*oses told Aaron
to take a jar and fill it with one
omer of manna and store it in the
presence of the L%%ORD%% to be kept
for the future generations.

E%%XODUS%% 16:33

Manna

Manna

Citrulus vulgaris

Melon

אבטיח

*W*e *could easily eat...*
melons...

NUMBERS 11:5

My beloved is to me a bag of Myrrh
that lies between my breasts.

The Song of Songs 1:13

Commiphora schimperi
Myrrh
מור

*T*hey reported to the angel of the Lord who stood among the myrtle trees, and said, "We have walked back and forth through the earth, and behold, all the earth is tranquil."

Zechariah 1:11

While the king sat at his table,
my perfume spread its fragrance.

The Song of Songs 1:12

Nardostachys jatamansi

Nard

נרד

*I*nstead *of the thorn the cypress tree will sprout; and instead of the nettle the myrtle will sprout.*

ISAIAH 55:13

Rebecca's nurse, Deborah, died, and she was buried under the oak below Beth-El, and Jacob named it Allon-bacuth.

GENESIS 35:8

Wail, you oaks of Bashan, for the strong forest has been cut down.

ZECHARIA 11:2

Olivae factus es
Olive tree
עץ זית

T**he Lord**
*named you,
green olive tree.*

J**eremiah 11:16**

T**hey said**
*to the olive tree,
"Be king over us."*

J**udges 9:9**

Cyperus papyrus

Papyrus

גמא

Put in your baggage ... balm and honey, gum tragacanth, myrrh, pistachio nuts and almonds.

Genesis 43:11

Pistachios

Pistacia vera

פיסטוקים

*J*acob
took fresh shoots
of poplar, almond,
and plane trees and
peeled off strips of bark
to expose the white of the
shoots.

GENESIS 30:37

Platanus orientalis
Plane
ערמון

Come my beloved,
lets go out to the fields,
To lie among the henna bushes.
Let's go early to the vineyards.
Let's see whether the vine has budded,
If its blossoms have opened,
If the pomegranates are in flower.
There I will give you my love.

The Song of Songs 7:12-13

Populus euphratica
Poplar
צפצפה

***B**y the rivers of Babylon,*
there we sat.
Yes, we wept, when we remembered Zion.
On the willows in that land,
we hung up our harps.

PSALMS 137:1-2

A *phrase well spoken*
is like golden apples in a setting of silver.

PROVERBS 25:11

Phragmites communis
Reed
קנה

*A*s *Egypt's canals dry up, the reeds and rushes will wither.*

Isaiah 19:6

*I*nstead *of reeds and rushes, grass will grow in the land.*

Isaiah 35:7

One of them
went out into the fields
to gather new shoots, and he
found a wild vine from which
he picked wild gourds,
gathering as many as he could carry
in his garment.
He came back and sliced them, and
put them in a pot without knowing
what they were.

2 KINGS 4:39

Crocus sativus

Saffron

כרכום

Spikenard and saffron,
Calamus and cinnamon,
with every kind of incense tree;
Myrrh and aloes,
with all the best perfumes,
A fountain of gardens,
A well of living waters.

The Song of Songs 4:14-15

Sage, Judean

Salvia judaica
מרווה יהודה

*M*ake a lampstand of pure gold. The stem and branches of the lampstand shall be hammered work. The cups, calyxes, and petals shall be of one piece. The lampstand shall have six branches, three from each side of it.

Exodus 25:31-32

Atriplex halimus
Saltwort
מלוח

*T*hey pluck
saltwort and wormwood;
and the roots of broom for warmth.

JOB 30:4

Styrax officinalis
Storax
לבנה

And the L ORD said to Moses, take fragrant spices, gum resin, aromatic shell, galbanum with pure frankincense together with the spices

E XODUS 30:34

*A*braham planted
a tamarisk tree at Beer-Sheba,
and there he called upon the Lord,
the Everlasting God, by name.

Genesis 21:33

Tamarix
Tamarisk
אשל

They gave Jacob
the foreign gods
that they had,
and the earrings
they were wearing,
and he buried them
under the terebinth tree
near Shechem.

Genesis 35:4

Pistacia palaestina
Terebinth
אלה

He has filled me with bitterness.
He has filled me with wormwood.

LAMENTATIONS 3:15

On the same night they should eat meat roasted on the fire and eat unleavened bread with bitter herbs.

EXODUS 12:8

Calycotome villosa
Thorn
חרול

*T*hey bray
among the bushes.
They are gathered together
under the nettles.
Outcasts from where people gather.

JOB 30:7-8

They will
come and settle in the rough wadis,
and in the crevices of the rocks
and in all of the thorn bushes and watering places.

ISAIAH 7:19

Instead of the thorn
the cypress tree will sprout.

ISAIAH 55:13

Alhagi maurorum
Thorn camel

נעצוץ

It is
the sound
of nations, a roaring like
a mighty stream. When he
shouts at them, they flee far
away, driven by the wind
like chaff in the hills and like
a tumbleweed before
the storm.

Isaiah 17:13

Gundelia tournefortii

Thorn gundelia

גלגל

***I**f
it has to be,
then put in your baggage
some of the best products
of the land as a gift for
the man…gum traga-
canth.*

Genesis 43:11

Astragalus gummifer
Tragacanth
נכאת

Juglans regia
Walnut
אגוז

***I** went down
into the nut tree grove,
to see the budding of the valley,
to see whether the vine blossomed,
and if the pomegranates were in flower.*

THE SONG OF SONGS 6:11

Ridolfia segetum
Weed ridolfia
באשה

If I have eaten
its fruit without payment,
or have caused its owners despair,
Let nettles grow there instead of wheat;
and stinkweed instead of barley.

JOB 31: 39-40

*T*ake
*for yourself also wheat,
barley, beans, lentils, millet,
and spelt; combine them in
a vessel and bake them into
bread.*

EZEKIEL 4:9

Triticum durum
Wheat
חטה

On
the first day
take the fruit
of the citrus trees, palm-
fonds, the branches of
leafy trees and willows
by the creek, and rejoice
before the L*ord* your God
for seven days.

Leviticus 23:40

Salix alba
Willow
ערבה

***I* will**
feed them with wormwood,
and make them drink bitter water;
because a godless spirit has spread
from the prophets of Jerusalem
to the whole land.

JEREMIAH 23:15

REFERENCES

Barton, Aaron. 1902. *A Sketch of Semitic Origins: Social and Religious.* New York: The Macmillan Company.

Goor, Asaph. "Five Fruits of the Holy Land" in *Economic Botany 1965-1967.* New York Botanical Garden.

Gardner, Jo Ann. 2014. *Seeds of Transcendence: Understanding the Hebrew Bible through Plants.* New York: Decalogue Books.

George, Andrew. 2016. *The Epic of Gilgamesh.* London: Penguin.

Janick, Jules. 2007. "Fruits of the Bible" in *HortScience* Vol. 42(5) August. https://hort.purdue.edu/newcrop/fruits%20of%20bible.pdf

Jensen, Hans Arne. 2012. *Plant World of the Bible.* Author House.

Josephus, Flavius. *The Jewish War. 1851.* Translated by Robert Trail. Oxford University. Digitized 2006.

Milton, John. 1667. *Paradise Lost.* Penguin Classics reprint 2003. London: Penguin.

Moldenke, Harold N. and Moldenke, Alma L. 1952. *Plants of the Bible.* New York: Dover Publication.

Musselman, Lytton John. 2007. *Figs, Dates, Laurel, and Myrrh.* Portland: Timber Press.

The Holy Scriptures According to the Masoretic Text. Philadelphia. JPS 1917

The biblical quotations are interpretations by the author based on the JPS 1917 Hebrew Bible (Tanakh).

About the Author

Gloria Abella Ballen is an artist and author creating award-winning art books such as *The Power of the Hebrew Alphabet* and *The New World Haggadah*, the latter with Ilan Stavans. Both titles won Best Book Awards with *The Power of the Hebrew Alphabet* winning multiple awards.

Abella Ballen has graduate degrees in art from SUNY-Buffalo and the National University in Mexico City and has done specialized studies on studio art and theory with Larry Rivers and John Cage.

She has exhibited internationally in individual and group shows and has received awards from the UNESCO prize in painting, the Latin American Graphics Biennial, National Endowment for the Arts, British Council and the Pan American Graphics Portfolio Award among others.

Her art is in the collections of museums, corporations and private individuals. She has been an international visiting artist in England at the University of Essex and the Camberwell School of Art (London), in China at the University of Xinjiang and in Israel at the Mishkan Omanim in Herzliya. Gloria has been a professor of art at universities in Puerto Rico, Colombia and the United States.

Abella Ballen currently lives in Santa Fe, New Mexico.

Gaon Books
www.gaonbooks.com
Garden of Eden: Plants of the Hebrew Bible. Gloria Abella Ballen.
Copyright 2020. All rights reserved. This publication is in copyright. Subject to statutory exception and to the provisions of relevant collective licensing agreements, no reproduction of any part may be made without the written permission of the Gaon Books, except for brief quotations included in analytical articles, chapters, and reviews. For permissions, group pricing, and other information contact
Gaon Books
P.O. Box 23924
Santa Fe, NM 87502
(admin@tolerancestudies.org).
www.tolerancestudies.org

Manufactured in the United States of America.

The paper used in this publication is acid free and meets all ANSI (American National Standards for Information Sciences) standards for archival quality paper. All wood product components used in this book are Sustainable Forest Initiative (SFI) certified.

Gaon Books is part of the Institute for Tolerance Studies
a not for profit organization (501-c-3) focused on
education about diversity,
focused on Jewish life, thought, and social roles.

Library of Congress Cataloging-in-Publication Data

Names: Ballen, Gloria Abella, author.
Title: Garden of Eden : Plants of the Hebrew Bible / Gloria Abella Ballen.
Description: Paper. | Santa Fe : Gaon Books, 2020. | Includes
   Bibliographical references. | Summary: "Historically the plants of the Bible have been of great interest for botanical studies, for their medicinal qualities, for cooking, for building gardens, for inspiration, as metaphors for teaching etc. The Bible narrative provides a social and symbolic meaning for the plants, although there has been difficulty in the translations and sometimes the names of precise species mentioned in the narrative are not known. The Hebrew Bible was written in Aramaic and Hebrew, it was first translated into Greek in the second century B.C.E., into Latin in the fourth century C.E., and later into the many languages of the world. The images in this book are of the plants mentioned in the narrative of the Tanakh (Hebrew Bible), their Hebrew name, and their scientific name in Latin. These images are accompanied by references from the biblical narrative. In the text I focused particularly on the five most mentioned plants: Fig, grape vine, olive, date palm and pomegranate"-- Provided by publisher.
Identifiers: LCCN 2020002188 | ISBN 9781935604860 (paperback)
Subjects: LCSH: Plants in the Bible. | Old Testament--Criticism,
   interpretation, etc.
Classification: LCC BS1199.P545 B35 2020 | DDC 221.8/58--dc23
LC record available at https://lccn.loc.gov/2020002188

When
*you come
to the Land,
you shall plant trees.*

LEVITICUS 19:23

www.ingramcontent.com/pod-product-compliance
Lightning Source LLC
Chambersburg PA
CBHW051549220426
43671CB00024B/2986